Bears, Bears Everywhe

Bears, bears everywhere.

Bears in pairs.

Bears, bears everywhere.

Bears in squares.

Furniture

Bears, bears everywhere.

Bears in chairs.

Bears, bears everywhere.

Bears climb stairs.

Bears, bears everywhere.
Bears pay fares.

Bears, bears everywhere.
Bears chase hares.

Bears, bears everywhere.
Bears eat pears.

Bears, bears everywhere.
Bears like fairs.

Bears, bears everywhere.
Bears can scare.

Bears, bears everywhere.
Bears curl hair.

Bears, bears everywhere.
I love my bears!